WHAT THE F*@# SHOULD I MAKE FOR DINNER?

The Answers to Life's Everyday Question (in 50 F*@#ing Recipes)

By Zach Golden

RUNNING PRESS
PHILADELPHIA · LONDON

To Sara, Oscar, and Dick Wolf

Books published by Running Press are available at special discounts
for bulk purchases in the United States by corporations, institutions, and
other organizations. For more information, please contact the Special
Markets Department at the Perseus Books Group, 2300 Chestnut
Street, Suite 200, Philadelphia, PA 19103, or call (800) 810-4145, ext.
5000, or e-mail special.markets@perseusbooks.com.

ISBN 978-0-7624-4177-8
Library of Congress Control Number: 2010941543

E-book ISBN 978-0-7624-4367-3

10
Digit on the right indicates the number of this printing

Cover and interior design by Jason Kayser
Edited by Kristen Green Wiewora
Typography: Helvetica

Running Press Book Publishers
2300 Chestnut Street
Philadelphia, PA 19103-4371

Visit us on the web!
www.runningpress.com

Introduction

Everyone needs to eat. I once heard of a man who baffled scientists with his reputed ability to forego eating for years on end, and well, that man is dead. And I can't imagine a less fun party guest. Some people say it's a drag to have to feed yourself, but plain and simple, those people are douchebags. But you, lover of all things gastronomic, you are a special breed. You possess the innate knowledge that feeding yourself, in addition to being a necessary activity, can be a hell of a lot of fun. But there is a dark side to being so wholly knowledgeable and handsome: choice. Choice, yes fucking choice: it's the cold bitch that stands between you and food coma. When I created the What the Fuck Should I Make for Dinner website (www.whatthefuckshouldimakefordinner.com), it was not out of benevolence. No sir or madam: it was out of malice for choice (did I mention choice is a bitch?), who, on many occasions has left me crying, shaking uncomfortably in the corner of my apartment, hungry and confused. And so, with this book, like the website, I hope that I can silence the voices in your head, even if only for a night, and tell your indecisive ass what the fuck to make for dinner.

Lessen vegetables' meat envy with some fucking Kale with Bacon

6 bacon slices, coarsely
   chopped
2 shallots, finely chopped
2 garlic cloves, minced

2 bunches kale, torn into
   1-inch pieces
2 cups chicken stock
2 teaspoons mustard seed

Cook the bacon perfectly in a sauté pan over medium heat. Do not fuck this up, or you will ruin the best part of the dish. Remember, without bacon this is just kale, and "just kale" can suck. When it's perfect, transfer the bacon to some paper towels, and let it hang out while the adults are talking. Don't you dare even think about draining the fat from the pan.

Add the shallots and garlic to the pan and sauté until tender, about 2 minutes. Add the kale, stock, and mustard seed, cook that shit for about 10 minutes, then lie to your kids about vegetables being not awful without the addition of meat.

Don't fucking like that?..........*Turn to page 10.*

Don't fucking eat meat?.........*Turn to page 90.*

5

Honor the mighty pig god with some fucking Prosciutto and Melon with Balsamic Glaze

½ cup balsamic vinegar
¼ cup dark brown sugar, packed
1 cantaloupe

2 tablespoons fresh mint
6 ounces prosciutto
Salt and pepper

Fucking *buongiorno*, epic pork and fruit dish. In a saucepan over high heat, bring the vinegar and sugar to a boil, then simmer until it's syrupy as fuck. Cut big cubes from the cantaloupe and chiffonade the mint.

Arrange the cantaloupe on a plate, place a halo of precious pig meat product on there, and sprinkle the mint on top. Season that shit with salt and pepper, then spoon on the balsamic glaze.

Don't fucking like that? .... *Turn to page 48.*

Don't fucking eat meat? .... *Turn to page 18.*

It's not cute when kids say "pasghetti," so teach them to say, make, and eat some fucking **Bucatini with Tomato, Mozzarella, and Basil**

1½ pounds plum tomatoes
8 ounces fresh mozzarella
   cheese
4 cloves garlic
½ cup fresh basil

3 tablespoons extra-virgin
   olive oil
Salt and pepper
12 ounces bucatini

Dice the tomatoes and mozzarella and throw that shit in a bowl. Mince the garlic and tear the basil, and add them to the mix with the olive oil and salt and pepper to taste. Don't pussyfoot around the salt and pepper, unless of course you have an affinity for shitty food; then please, pussyfoot away.

    Let the mixture sit for an hour. Cook the pasta in heavily salted water until al dente: that's Italian for "not total shit." Then, add to the tomato mixture, toss, and serve.

Don't fucking like that? .... *Turn to page 32.*

Not a fucking vegetarian? .... *Turn to page 12.*

I'd say eat shit, but that wouldn't be helpful, so why don't you make some fucking **Braised Lamb Shanks**

6 tablespoons extra-virgin
  olive oil, divided
6 lamb shanks
Salt and pepper
3 ribs celery, diced
2 carrots, diced
1 large white onion, diced

5 sprigs fresh thyme
1 whole head of garlic,
  cut in half crosswise
3 cups red wine
2 cups beef stock
2 cups chicken stock

Preheat your oven to 325°F. Put a Dutch oven over high heat and add 3 tablespoons of oil. Season the lamb shanks with a shitload of salt and pepper, and add to the pan. Sear the shit out of the lamb shanks until they are browned all over and the fucking neighbors can smell them, but don't give them any. Remove the shanks for a few minutes. Add 3 more tablespoons of oil in the pot and add the diced celery, carrot, and onion. Cook them until they're fucking soft and sweet, about 10 minutes. Add the thyme and garlic, and cook for 2 more minutes. Add the wine and both stocks, raise the heat to high, and bring that shit to a boil. Put the lamb shanks back in the pot, seal that shit with some aluminum foil or a lid, and put it in the oven. You didn't forget to preheat the oven did you? Goddamn right you didn't. Cook that shit for 3 to 4 hours, uncovering after an hour. Skim the fat, serve, and be hailed as a god or at the very least a demigod.

Don't fucking like that? .... *Turn to page 16.*
Don't fucking eat meat? .... *Turn to page 72.*

Your indecision is truly disgusting, but I digress: cook up some fucking Brisket

A brisket, about 6 pounds
6 large cloves of garlic,
    minced
2 sprigs fresh thyme
2 sprigs fresh tarragon
2 sprigs fresh rosemary
Salt and pepper
2 tablespoons extra-virgin
    olive oil

4 large Vidalia onions,
    roughly chopped
4 carrots, roughly chopped
1 cup beef stock
3 tablespoons tomato paste
2 cups dry red wine

Preheat your oven to 300°F. Season your brisket on all sides with garlic, thyme, tarragon, rosemary, and a fucking shitload of salt and pepper. Add oil to a big oven-safe Dutch oven, and get that thing fucking hot. One step below, "What's that? Oh, it's the smoke alarm" hot. Add the brisket, brown it on both sides, about 4 minutes each. Then add the onions and carrots. Place everything in the oven uncovered for 1 hour. Now that you've got a fucking hour to kill, get a bowl and combine beef stock, tomato paste, and the wine. Whisk it until it's smooth as balls, and add it to the pan after the hour. Cover the pan and cook for 3½ more hours, plenty of time to enjoy the rest of the bottle of wine. When it's done, slice it thin and eat it.

Don't fucking like that? . . . . *Turn to page 98.*

Don't fucking eat meat? . . . . *Turn to page 8.*

13

Eat my balls, and if that doesn't sound appetizing, try some fucking Roast Chicken

A chicken, 2 to 5 pounds
1 tablespoon fresh parsley
1 tablespoon fresh thyme
1 tablespoon fresh rosemary
½ cup unsalted butter,
    divided

Salt and pepper
1 lemon, halved
2 large yellow onions
2 carrots
2 ribs celery

Preheat your oven to 400°F. Now deep breath, Sport, you got this one. Rinse your chicken with cold water, remove all the fucking giblets, and pat it dry. Cut your herbs until they are fine and tiny. Starting at the neck, stuff thin pats of butter (about ¼ cup) under the skin all over that fucking bird. Melt the rest of the butter and brush it on the chicken, then make it rain herbs on that bitch. Season with a shitload of salt and pepper, and stuff the cavity with the lemon. Now dice the onions, carrots, and celery; put them on the bottom of a roasting pan and put the chicken on top. Cook the chicken until a thermometer reads 160°F, about 30 to 75 minutes depending on the size of the bird, then pull that shit out and let it sit for a few minutes, this will bring the internal temperature to 165°F. Serve and demand the Pope's nose; it's the fucking cook's prerogative.

Don't fucking like that? . . . . *Turn to page 78.*
Don't fucking eat meat? . . . . *Turn to page 30.*

Feel ashamed of your childhood ignorance with some fucking Brussels Sprouts

1 pound Brussels sprouts

¼ cup extra-virgin olive oil

Salt and pepper

3 shallots, finely chopped, divided

2 teaspoons mustard seed

4 ounces bacon, diced

¼ cup white wine, preferably Chardonnay

1 tablespoon Dijon mustard

Preheat your oven to 400°F. Halve sprouts. Rinse em' off, but don't fucking peel that shit: they're going into a scorching hot oven, don't be a pussy. Put them in a low-sided roasting pan and olive oil, salt, and pepper the shit out of them. Add half of the shallots and the mustard seed. Roast the sprouts for about 30 minutes. Pull them out when they are tender and taste good. Get a sauté pan hot over medium-high heat. Add the bacon, and cook until perfectly crisp. Don't fuck this up. Take the bacon out of the pan; reserve the fat. Throw the remaining shallots into the same pan, and crank the heat. Sauté in the bacon fat for about 4 minutes, until caramelized. Add the white wine and Dijon mustard, whisk the fuck out of it, and add more salt and pepper. Dress the Brussels sprouts with the sauce in the pan, drop that bacon on there too, and toss that shit.

Don't fucking like that? .... *Turn to page 78.*

Don't fucking eat meat? .... *Turn to page 54.*

Make your crunchy-granola ass some fucking

Avocado, Fennel, and Citrus Salad

1 orange
1 grapefruit
3 tablespoons red wine
   vinegar
2 teaspoons fennel seeds,
   crushed
¼ teaspoon salt

3 tablespoons extra-virgin
   olive oil
Salt and pepper
2 large avocados
1 fennel bulb, thinly sliced
1 cup pea sprouts
1 shallot, minced

Take your orange and grate some zest from it; set that shit aside. Suprême the orange and grapefruit. What, you don't know what that means, Asshole? It means take your knife, peel that shit, then cut between membranes of the fruit to release the segments, and don't forget to save the fucking juice. Don't make me explain that shit again. Whisk together the vinegar, fennel seeds, salt, orange zest, and about 1 tablespoon each of the reserved orange and grapefruit juices. Whisk in the oil nice and slow, and season that shit to taste. Slice the avocado nice and thin, don't get all ham-fisted on that bitch. Toss the sliced fennel, sprouts, and minced shallots in the dressing. Spoon some dressing on the avocado, orange, and grapefruit. Plate it however the fuck you feel, and consider adding some meat to your next meal.

Don't fucking like that?.........*Turn to page 56.*
Not a fucking vegetarian? ....*Turn to page 34.*

Induce food coma with some fucking Pad Thai

1 (8–ounce) package rice
   noodles
1 chicken breast, thinly sliced
3 teaspoons peanut oil
1 head baby bok choy, leaves
   separated
3 tablespoons fish sauce
1 teaspoon peanut butter

½ teaspoon sugar
2 eggs
½ package firm tofu
1 cup bean sprouts
3 scallions, chopped
1 lime, cut in wedges
3 teaspoons crushed peanuts

Look at you, Tough Guy, making something from Thailand. Looks like I was wrong about you. In a large saucepan, bring four cups of water to a boil, and cook rice noodles until just softened, about 2 minutes. Drain. In a wok or deep pan, cook your chicken in the oil over medium heat, about a minute per side. Add the bok choy leaves to the pan and cook for a minute more, then add the fish sauce, peanut butter, and sugar. Smell that? Yeah, that's fucking Pad Thai. Make a well in the center of the wok, crack the eggs into the center and scramble until softly cooked. Add the tofu, sprouts, and scallions. Stir that shit up; if you've got a wok, get all fancy and toss that bitch around. Add the cooked rice noodles to the wok, heat through, remove from the heat, and serve. Garnish with lime wedges and crushed peanuts and say fucking "mai-pen-rai" to all of your adoring fans yelling "kob-khun."

Don't fucking like that? . . . . *Turn to page 92.*
Don't fucking eat meat? . . . . *Turn to page 60.*

Feed your mouthface with some fucking Veal Stew

2 pounds veal
Salt and pepper
⅓ cup flour
¼ cup extra-virgin olive oil
1 tablespoon butter
2 medium white onions, diced
4 ribs celery, diced
2 large carrots, diced

½ cup dry white wine
1½ cups chicken stock
1½ cups crushed tomatoes
2 tablespoons tomato paste
¼ teaspoon red pepper flakes
2 tablespoons lemon rind
2 teaspoons rosemary
2 teaspoons parsley

Do a large fucking dice on your veal; get that shit into 1½-inch cubes and season with salt and pepper. Dredge the veal in flour. Heat the olive oil and butter in a large skillet. Get that pan hot as fuck, and brown the veal cubes all over. Transfer veal to a big fucking stockpot. Reserve the fat in the skillet and add the diced onion, celery, and carrot, and let that shit absorb some delicious meat flavor for about 2 minutes. Make it a proper party by pouring in the wine and cooking until it evaporates. Add the stock, tomatoes, tomato paste, and red pepper, and stir that bitch up. Pour the mixture over the meat, bring to a boil, and cover. Simmer over medium heat for about 45 minutes, or until that meat is tender as balls and mouth-achingly delicious. Be a good cook and top that shit with gremolata by finely chopping the lemon rind, rosemary, and parsley together. Look at you, making something of yourself.

Don't fucking like that? .... *Turn to page 68.*
Don't fucking eat meat? .... *Turn to page 96.*

It's a party
in your mouth,
and everybody's
coming, so
why don't you
cook up
some fucking
Pasta
Carbonara

1 pound spaghetti
2 tablespoons extra-virgin
   olive oil
8 slices bacon, diced
1 yellow onion, diced
1 clove garlic, minced

Salt and pepper
½ cup grated Parmesan
   cheese
2 tablespoons minced
   fresh parsley
4 egg yolks

Bring a large pot of water to a boil, and salt the shit out of it; make it taste like the fucking sea. Cook the pasta until *al dente*; don't fuck this up unless you like ruining food. Drain it, and toss it with some olive oil while it rests. In a large skillet, cook the diced bacon until slightly crisp, then set aside. Respect the bacon. Add 1 tablespoon of olive oil to the bacon fat in the same skillet, and add the diced onion. Allow the lowly onion to bask in the glory of the bacon over medium-high heat until that shit is just starting to caramelize, then add the minced garlic and cook 1 minute more. Throw the bacon back in the pan and add the pasta; toss it to coat and heat through. Add some more fucking olive oil if it's dry, but it shouldn't be if you haven't fucked it up. This would be a good time to salt and pepper that hot bitch to taste. For serving, place the pasta in a bowl and top with some Parmesan cheese and parsley. Add a fucking egg yolk to each serving, stir it up, and eat that shit immediately. Commence food coma.

Don't fucking like that? .... *Turn to page 36.*
Don't fucking eat meat? .... *Turn to page 26.*

Don't fuck up some fucking Red Flannel Hash

¾ pound red-skinned
   potatoes, peeled
1 large sweet potato, peeled
½ pound beets, peeled
¼ cup extra-virgin olive oil

Salt and pepper
4 eggs
2 tablespoons butter
¼ cup chopped fresh
   parsley

You're gonna roast the shit out of some vegetables, so preheat your oven to 375°F. Do a large dice on the peeled potatoes, sweet potato, and beets, then give 'em a golden shower of olive oil. Salt and pepper to taste, which means a shitload unless your palate sucks. Throw that shit in the oven and roast until tender, about 45 minutes.

Cook up some eggs however the fuck you like them. Sunny-side up is the hot shit, but if you've got a thing for flipping them, then by all means. Use butter when you cook your eggs—none of that fucking no-stick spray bullshit—and season them with salt and pepper. Plate the roasted hash, and top with parsley and a fucking perfectly cooked egg. Eat and espouse the glory of breakfast for dinner.

Don't fucking like that? .... *Turn to page 80.*

Not a fucking vegetarian? .... *Turn to page 28.*

Classily partake of some fucking Grilled Swordfish with Pineapple Salsa

4 eight-ounce swordfish
  steaks
2 tablespoons extra-virgin
  olive oil
Salt and pepper

1 cup cherry tomatoes
1 cup diced fresh pineapple
1 small red onion, diced
1 bunch fresh cilantro
1 lime

Get your grill or broiler ready with medium-high heat; make sure that shit is clean so your fish won't stick. Drizzle some olive oil on the swordfish, and salt and pepper both sides. Grill the fish for about 4 minutes a side until it's firm—but a couple hundred miles away from dry.

Halve the cherry tomatoes and throw them in a bowl with the pineapple and red onion. Finely slice the cilantro, fucking stems and all, and add it with the juice of one lime and salt and pepper. Serve the salsa on top of the fish. That was fucking easy.

Don't fucking like that? .... *Turn to page 62.*

Don't fucking eat meat? .... *Turn to page 66.*

Feast your eyes, and subsequently your mouth, on some fucking Eggs with Ricotta and Chives

4 large eggs
1 tablespoon chopped fresh chives, divided
3 tablespoons butter, divided

Salt and pepper
½ cup fresh ricotta cheese
Baguette slices
1 clove garlic, halved

Motherfucking breakfast for dinner: if you don't like it, I don't fucking like you. Whisk the eggs and most of the chives until that shit is blended proper. Melt 2 tablespoons of butter in a nonstick pan over medium heat, and add the eggs. Stir that shit up; I don't need to fucking tell you how to make scrambled eggs. Season with salt and pepper, and don't fucking overcook them. Pull off the heat and add the ricotta, stirring until it's incorporated.

Toast the baguette slices, rub them with garlic, butter them, and throw some of the eggs on top. Make it look real fucking fancy with some more chives, and then eat it.

Don't fucking like that? .... *Turn to page 84.*
Not a fucking vegetarian? .... *Turn to page 4.*

Existentially lose yourself in some fucking Beet Salad with Chèvre

4 beets
¼ cup extra-virgin olive oil
¼ cup sherry vinegar
1 tablespoon honey
1 teaspoon Dijon mustard
1 teaspoon toasted
    sesame oil

Salt and pepper
2 cups arugula
1 fennel bulb, sliced
2 plum tomatoes, diced
4 ounces goat cheese

Preheat your oven to 375°F. Wrap your beets loosely in foil. Roast the shit out of them until they're nice and tender, about an hour. Let them cool, peel them, and then dice 'em up. Prepare for your kitchen to look like a *Law and Order* murder scene. For the fucking dressing, blend the olive oil, vinegar, honey, mustard, and sesame oil until it's all dressing-like. Season with salt and pepper.

Combine the beets, arugula, fennel, and tomatoes in a bowl, dress them to your liking, and toss. Add some fucking goat cheese, season with some more salt and pepper, and eat that shit up.

Don't fucking like that? . . . . *Turn to page 88.*
Not a fucking vegetarian? . . . . *Turn to page 50.*

You like it when I talk dirty? Oh yeah, then you're gonna make some fucking Escarole, Sausage, and White Bean Soup

4 sweet Italian chicken
sausages
2 tablespoons extra-virgin
olive oil
2 cloves garlic, minced
2 heads of escarole, roughly
chopped

4 cups chicken stock
1 cup canned and drained
cannellini beans
1 teaspoon red pepper
flakes
Salt and pepper

This is so easy even you can't fuck it up. Cook the sausage however the hell you want; set it aside. In a large sauté pan, heat the oil up and drop in the minced garlic. Cook it until it's brown, but don't burn it, or it will be fucking bitter and awful and you will have failed. Drop the escarole in the pan, then add the stock. Let the greens cook down for about 4 minutes, then add the beans and red pepper flakes, and serve it with some of the sausage. Don't forget to season your food. Molto fucking benne.

Don't fucking like that? . . . . *Turn to page 44.*

Don't fucking eat meat? . . . . *Turn to page 53.*

Satisfy your meat tooth with some fucking Grilled Skirt Steak with Chimichurri

3 tablespoons red-wine
   vinegar
4 cloves garlic, minced
½ teaspoon red pepper
   flakes
½ bay leaf

¼ cup extra-virgin olive oil
½ cup finely chopped fresh
   flat-leaf parsley
A fucking skirt steak
Salt and pepper

For the chimichurri, stir together the fucking vinegar, 2 tablespoons water, garlic, red pepper flakes, and bay leaf. Whisk in the oil and the parsley, let that shit stand for an hour, and throw out the fucking bay leaf.

For the steak, get your grill fucking hot. I refuse to tell you how to do that part. Coat your steak with lots of salt and pepper; don't fucking pussyfoot around your seasoning, Champ. Grill that shit until perfectly done the way you want it. I'm not a fucking mind reader, but if it's past medium, put the fucking book down and have a long, hard look at yourself. Slice the steak against the grain, put it on a plate—or if you want to be fancy, a serving platter—spoon some chimichurri on top, and yell "Booya!" Or don't yell booya: either way.

Don't fucking like that? . . . . *Turn to page 42.*
Don't fucking eat meat? . . . . *Turn to page 76.*

It's about to get classy up in this bitch, because somebody's cooking up some fucking Scallops with Swiss Chard

2 bunches Swiss chard
2 tablespoons extra-virgin
olive oil, divided
Juice of 1 lemon

Salt and fresh cracked pepper
1 pound sea scallops
3 tablespoons unsalted
butter

This dish will get you fucked, plain and simple. Bring heavily salted water to a boil in a large stock pot; make that shit taste like the sea. Remove the stems from the Swiss chard, chop it, and add the leaves to the boiling water. Let that Euro-chard boil for 2 minutes, and then transfer immediately to an ice bath. Squeeze out any excess water. Heat 1 tablespoon olive oil in a sauté pan—get that shit hot as balls—and add the chard, lemon juice, and some salt and pepper. Cook, then put on a plate.

Put a sauté pan over high heat, and add the rest of the oil. Get the pan hot—to be precise, "Oh shit, the oil just started fucking smoking so now I know the pan is properly hot and I will not let the oil smoke anymore" hot. Coat the scallops on both sides with salt and pepper. If you under-season, you may as well eat shit, and don't over season either: just fucking get it right. Put the scallops in the aforementioned hot pan and cook 2 minutes per side. Before removing from the pan, add the butter to that shit, and spoon over each scallop. Don't worry, they fucking like it. Serve, eat, and get fucked.

Don't fucking like that? .... *Turn to page 20.*
Don't fucking eat meat? .... *Turn to page 90.*

You ruin most everything you touch, so let's not fuck up some fucking **Scallop Ceviche**

1 cup cherry tomatoes
½ mango
½ red onion
¾ cup fresh cilantro
2 serrano chiles, minced

1 cup fresh orange juice
⅓ cup fresh lemon juice
⅓ cup fresh lime juice
1 pound bay scallops
Salt and pepper

You can't fuck this one up, seriously, not possible. Time for some fucking *mise en place*. Quarter the cherry tomatoes. Dice the mango and red onion, then chop most of the cilantro. Throw all that in a bowl along with the rest of the shit, and fucking season it. Eat with your eyes and garnish with some more cilantro. And don't give me any of that, "But I don't like cilantro," bullshit. It's fucking delicious. Let everything sit tight for 10 minutes, then dig in, Sport.

Don't fucking like that? .... *Turn to page 24.*
Don't fucking eat meat? .... *Turn to page 18.*

Is it hot in here? Nope, it's just these fucking delicious Mussels with Green Peppercorn Sauce

2 tablespoons unsalted
    butter
2 large shallots, diced
1½ teaspoons crushed dried
    green peppercorns
1 cup Chardonnay

4 pounds mussels
½ cup heavy cream
2 tablespoons chopped
    flat-leaf parsley, divided
Some fucking bread for
    serving

In a big pot, heat the butter. Add the diced shallots and cook until translucent, then add the crushed peppercorns. Stir that shit up for a couple minutes. Add the booze and bring it to a simmer; don't over-boil it, bitch. Crank the heat, drop in the mussels, and let the booze loosen 'em up like a 16-year-old at a frat party. Tell them you love them, and they'll let you do whatever you want. You'll know they're ready when they open up. And toss any unopened ones—unless you like dying, then keep them. Add the cream, throw in most of the parsley, and stir that shit. Top with more parsley when you serve it, and get some fucking bread ready: you're gonna like the sauce.

Don't fucking like that? .... *Turn to page 94.*
Don't fucking eat meat? .... *Turn to page 32.*

Lessen your mother's shame with some fucking Linguine with Heirloom Tomatoes and Anchovy

12 ounces linguine
¼ cup extra-virgin olive oil,
    divided
6 anchovy fillets, mashed
3 cloves garlic, minced and
    divided
1 cup coarse fresh
    breadcrumbs

1 pound heirloom tomatoes,
    diced
1 cup torn fresh basil
½ cup grated Parmesan
    cheese
Salt and pepper

Cook the linguine in balls-salty water until perfectly al dente. Reserve about ½ cup of that starchy water. Heat 2 tablespoons of olive oil in a sauté pan over medium heat and add the anchovy, half of the garlic, and the breadcrumbs. Cook about 5 minutes, tossing that shit occasionally; don't worry, they like to be thrown around. Set the mixture aside. In the same pan, add the remaining oil and garlic and the tomatoes. Cook that shit over high heat for about 4 minutes. Add the linguine, basil, Parmesan cheese, and some pasta water to the tomato mixture until it's delicious and sauce-like. Toss that shit like it's your first time, add half of the breadcrumb mixture, and fucking season it. Serve with more of the breadcrumb mixture on top.

Don't fucking like that? .... *Turn to page 74.*
Don't fucking eat meat? .... *Turn to page 72.*

45

Pretend you don't suck at cooking and well, life, and cook up some fucking Clams with Andouille Sausage

2 tablespoons unsalted
   butter
2 large shallots, diced
8 ounces andouille sausage,
   sliced
2 poblano chiles, diced
1 yellow bell pepper, diced
1 red bell pepper, diced

4 pounds Manila clams
½ cup dry sherry
½ cup heavy whipping cream
½ cup chopped fresh
   cilantro, divided
2 teaspoons sherry wine
   vinegar
Salt and pepper

Heat up some butter in a big fucking pot. Add the shallots, and let that shit cook for a few minutes. Add the sausage and all the diced peppers. Let 'em sauté for about 8 minutes. This shit is like children: don't leave it unattended.

Add the clams, sherry, and some cream. Cook until the clams fucking open up like your drunk uncle at Thanksgiving, about 5 minutes. Toss any clams that don't open. Top that shit with some cilantro and the vinegar, then season that motherfucker and stir. This shit is naked without more cilantro, so unless you're one of those fucking nature perverts, add some more.

Don't fucking like that? .... *Turn to page 6.*
Don't fucking eat meat? .... *Turn to page 8.*

Finally, you've found something easier than your little sister. Now cook up some fucking **Brined Pork Chops with Radicchio**

Salt

1½ tablespoons sugar

4 pork chops

Cracked pepper

1 head radicchio

1 head Belgian endive

3 tablespoons extra-virgin olive oil, divided

3 tablespoons chopped fresh parsley

Mix 1½ cups water, a bunch of salt, and the sugar in a plastic bag. Add the pork and brine for about 20 minutes. Get your grill hot as shit. After your swine is brined, remove, pat dry, and season with fresh cracked pepper.

Halve your radicchio and endive, douse in 2 tablespoons olive oil, and season the fuck out of 'em with salt and pepper. Grill the meat and vegetables until the pork has an internal temperature of 145°F and the vegetables are soft and browned. Top all that shit with parsley and another tablespoon of olive oil, then celebrate your fucking place in the food chain.

Don't fucking like that? . . . . *Turn to page 14.*

Don't fucking eat meat? . . . . *Turn to page 30.*

Feast upon some fucking Lamb Sausage with Figs and Greens

¼ cup extra-virgin olive oil, divided

2 tablespoons balsamic vinegar

1 tablespoon Dijon mustard

Salt and pepper

6 lamb sausages

1 red onion, sliced

A shitload of baby arugula

½ cup chèvre

6 fresh figs, quartered

¼ cup fresh mint

Sarah Palin's political stunt baby could make this dish, so you should have no trouble. Whisk together 3 tablespoons of oil, the vinegar, and the mustard, and season it with salt and pepper. Cook your sausages and onion however the fuck you want; grill them if you know what's up, then slice the sausage. Toss the greens with the dressing, and season with some more salt and pepper. Throw some greens on the plate; top with the sliced sausage and onions, goat cheese, figs, and whole mint leaves. Season with some more salt and pepper, top with the rest of the olive oil, and fucking enjoy

Don't fucking like that? .... *Turn to page 58.*

Don't fucking eat meat? .... *Turn to page 54.*

Commit crustacean genocide with some classy fucking Steamed Lobster with Saffron Butter

2 lobsters
1 tablespoon heavy cream
1 teaspoon lemon juice
½ cup butter, cut into
tablespoons

1 teaspoon saffron
Salt and pepper

This shit is classy and easy as fuck. In a stockpot, bring water to a boil. Ignore your fucking conscience: add the lobsters, cover, and steam until the shells are pink, about 12 minutes. In a small saucepan over medium-low heat, add the cream and lemon juice. Add the butter in pieces, whisking constantly. Add the saffron and some salt and pepper, and voilà, your fucking dinner is ready. If you respect yourself, don't wear a bib.

Don't fucking like that? .... *Turn to page 100.*
Don't fucking eat meat? .... *Turn to page 56.*

Dream of meatier meals of yesteryear over some fucking Watermelon and Feta Salad

1 medium watermelon
6 ounces feta cheese,
   crumbled
¼ cup fresh mint

2 teaspoons balsamic
   vinegar
Salt and pepper

This bitch tastes like summer and is easier than your high school prom date. Do a big fucking dice on the watermelon, and add the crumbled feta. Hand-tear or chiffonade the mint, add it to the mixture, and add the balsamic vinegar. Salt and pepper that shit to taste, and boom—it's fucking summer in your mouth.

Don't fucking like that? .... *Turn to page 60.*
Not a fucking vegetarian? .... *Turn to page 40.*

53

Your debatably vegetarian life-self should make some fucking Fennel Salad

1 fennel bulb, thinly sliced
3 ribs celery, thinly sliced
¼ cup pumpkin seeds
2 tablespoons extra-virgin
  olive oil
1 tablespoon Dijon mustard

1 tablespoon honey
1 tablespoon lemon juice
Salt and pepper
¾ cup grated Parmesan
  cheese

Fennel is by far the vegetable best equipped to survive a prison shanking, so surely it's good enough for your salad. Combine the fennel and celery in a large bowl. Toast and salt the fuck out of some pumpkin seeds, and add those, too.

In a small bowl, whisk the oil, mustard, honey, and lemon juice, and season with salt and pepper. Get all salady up in this piece and toss the shit out of it, then top with some grated Parmesan cheese.

Don't fucking like that? ....*Turn to page 96.*
Not a fucking vegetarian? ....*Turn to page 38.*

Prove your high school guidance counselor wrong, and don't fuck up some Frisée and Apple Salad

4½ tablespoons lemon juice
1½ shallots, finely chopped
½ teaspoon grated lemon
    zest
4½ tablespoons extra-virgin
    olive oil
Salt and pepper

2 heads frisée
2 heads Belgian endive,
    julienned
2 Fuji apples, diced
9 radishes, halved
3 tablespoons chopped
    fresh parsley

A salad for dinner? Yeah, pipe down, Asshole. Combine the lemon juice, shallots, and lemon zest. Whisk in the oil a little bit at a time; easy, Sailor. Season the dressing with some salt and pepper. Check it, which means tasting that shit, and make sure it doesn't suck in any capacity.

Combine the frisée, endive, apples, radishes, and parsley in a large bowl. Add the dressing, toss, season some more, and fucking serve it.

Don't fucking like that? .... *Turn to page 26.*

Not a fucking vegetarian? .... *Turn to page 82.*

You won't not eat some fucking Salmon with Hoisin and Citrus

2 heads of baby bok choy
1 pound salmon
Salt and pepper
2 tablespoons fresh orange juice
1 scallion, chopped
1 tablespoon hoisin

1 teaspoon minced fresh ginger
¾ teaspoon coriander seeds
½ teaspoon grated orange zest
¼ cup chopped fresh cilantro

Preheat your oven to 425°F. Pull the bok choy leaves apart and arrange in little nests on a sheet pan lined with aluminum foil. Top the nests with the salmon, which you diligently seasoned with some salt and pepper, ain't that right, Sport?

In a bowl, mix the orange juice, scallion, hoisin, ginger, coriander seeds, and orange zest. Sprinkle on the fish, then wrap that shit up tight in the foil, sealing it completely: no holes, no problem. Bake until the salmon is perfectly medium-rare, about 10 to 12 minutes, then open up the foil, make it rain chopped cilantro, and serve.

Don't fucking like that? .... *Turn to page 86.*

Don't fucking eat meat? .... *Turn to page 80.*

Keep it gangster with some fucking Haricots Verts and Brussels Sprouts

1 pound haricots verts
3 tablespoons extra-virgin
  olive oil
1 teaspoon red pepper
  flakes

1½ pounds Brussels
  sprouts, halved
Salt and pepper
2 bunches fresh mint,
  chopped

This is easy as fuck and vegetarian as fuck, so win-win if that's your thing. Blanch the haricots verts in balls-salty water, about 1 minute. Drain that shit.

In a sauté pan over high heat, get the oil hot, and add the red pepper flakes and Brussels sprouts. Season the fuck out of the sprouts and sauté until tender, about 6 minutes. Add the haricots verts and sauté for 2 more minutes, then add the mint and toss. Check the seasoning, and if all's good in the hood, fucking eat it.

Don't fucking like that? . . . . *Turn to page 66.*

Not a fucking vegetarian? . . . . *Turn to page 64.*

Get mouth-deep on some fucking Jambalaya

1 pound pork andouille
    sausage, sliced
1 tablespoon extra-virgin
    olive oil
2 green bell peppers, diced
2 ribs celery, diced
1 white onion, diced

3 scallions, chopped
2 cloves garlic, minced
Salt and pepper
1 pound long-grain
    white rice
4 large tomatoes, diced

In a large stockpot over high heat, cook the sausage in the oil until browned, about 5 minutes. Pull that shit out of the pot and reserve. Toss in the peppers, celery, onion, scallions, and garlic. Season that shit with some salt and pepper and let it caramelize, about 10 minutes. Stir in the rice, sausage, tomatoes, 3½ cups water, and more salt and pepper. Use your taste buds: it should taste like Bourbon Street in your mouth, but without the drunken co-eds and regret. Let it come to a boil, then reduce the heat and simmer with a lid until the rice is tender, about 25 minutes. Let that shit sit for about 10 minutes before you fucking serve it, then game on.

Don't fucking like that? .... *Turn to page 52.*
Don't fucking eat meat? .... *Turn to page 84.*

Cure your mouth's post-traumatic stress disorder with some fucking Sirloin with Pomegranate Glaze

A big fucking sirloin steak
Salt and pepper
2 teaspoons chopped fresh
  rosemary
3 tablespoons extra-virgin
  olive oil, divided

1 cup pomegranate juice
4 teaspoons brown sugar
2½ teaspoons balsamic
  vinegar, divided
4 cups arugula

Season your meat with a shitload of salt and pepper and the rosemary. Get a sauté pan hot as fuck and add 2 tablespoons of oil. Add the steak and cook until it's perfect, about 4 minutes per side for medium-rare. When it's cooked, let it rest; don't fucking slice it to check it. Seriously, don't. I'll come to your house and get you with a knife.

In a saucepan, add the pomegranate juice, brown sugar, and 2 teaspoons of vinegar. Let it boil, then simmer until it's reduced to a syrup. Toss some arugula with the remainder of the olive oil and balsamic vinegar, and season with salt and pepper. Slice the steak after its much-needed rest, drizzle on some of the glaze, and top with the salad of arugula.

Don't fucking like that? . . . . *Turn to page 70.*

Don't fucking eat meat? . . . . *Turn to page 88.*

Attempt not to disfigure yourself while making some fucking Sautéed Kale

2 bunches kale
¼ cup extra-virgin olive oil, divided
2 shallots, finely chopped
4 cloves garlic, minced
2 tablespoons chopped drained capers
1 teaspoon red pepper flakes
Salt and pepper

Get some salty-ass water boiling in a stockpot. Add the kale and cook until it's almost tender, about 8 minutes. Drain it, then drop it in an ice bath or cold running water. Drain it again, then chop it up. Not too small, Chief—you wouldn't want to fuck this up now, would you?

Get half of the oil hot in a large skillet over medium-high heat. Add the shallots, and sauté until they start to caramelize, about 3 minutes. Add the garlic, capers, and red pepper flakes, and cook for 1 minute more. Add the kale to the pan, toss it a few times, season it with some salt and pepper and some more olive oil, and fucking eat that shit.

Don't fucking like that? . . . . *Turn to page 53.*

Not a fucking vegetarian? . . . . *Turn to page 22.*

Prove your ability to follow linear instructions with some fucking Grilled Lamb Meatballs

1 pound ground lamb
2 cloves garlic, minced
1 small yellow onion, minced
1 egg
1 teaspoon ground cumin
1 teaspoon smoked paprika

2 tablespoons chopped
    parsley
2 tablespoons cilantro
Salt and pepper
2 tablespoons extra-virgin
    olive oil

Get your grill hot as fuck. Mix the lamb, garlic, onion, egg, cumin, paprika, parsley, cilantro, and some salt and pepper together. Get your hands in there and mix some shit up. Form some meatballs, but don't make them too small, or they'll fucking dry out on the grill—and that would suck.

Brush the meatballs with the oil and grill them until they feel firm when touched, but don't get too touchy. I'm fucking watching you, pervert.

Don't fucking like that? . . . . *Turn to page 10.*
Don't fucking eat meat? . . . . *Turn to page 76.*

If you are a dude, wallow in accolades; if you are a shewoman, revel in the expectation that you won't fuck up some fucking Striped Bass with Lemon and Mint

1 whole striped bass
Salt and pepper
1 lemon, sliced and divided
¼ cup fresh mint, divided
5 tablespoons extra-virgin
    olive oil

½ cup chopped scallions
    (about 2 to 3)
1 tablespoon lemon juice
2 teaspoons oregano
2 cloves garlic, minced

Turn your broiler on. Cut some slits in your fish, and season it with salt and pepper inside and out. Don't be afraid to get your fingers in there. Stuff most of the lemon and half of the mint leaves inside the cavity.

In a blender, purée the olive oil, scallions, the rest of the mint, lemon juice, oregano, and garlic. Get that shit real smooth-like, and spoon some of it over the fish and inside the cavity. Don't fucking use it all—easy, Cowboy.

Cook the fish until firm and the skin is crisp, about 4 minutes per side. Serve with some sliced lemon, the rest of the sauce, and a marginally larger sense of self-worth.

Don't fucking like that? .... *Turn to page 48.*
Don't fucking eat meat? .... *Turn to page 90.*

Honor the king of vegetables and make some fucking Broccoli Rabe

A shitload of broccoli rabe

¼ cup extra-virgin olive oil

4 cloves garlic, minced

1 teaspoon red pepper flakes

1 lemon

Salt and pepper

If you're going to have the audacity to eat a fully vegetarian meal, at least have the audacity to make it fucking awesome. Blanch the broccoli rabe in a large pot of heavily salted boiling water for about 2 minutes. Transfer immediately to an ice bath, and then drain that shit.

In a large sauté pan, heat the olive oil over medium-high heat and add the garlic; cook for about a minute. Add the broccoli rabe and fucking toss it. Add the red pepper flakes, the juice of the lemon, and salt and pepper to taste. See? A vegetarian dish doesn't taste so fucking bad.

Don't fucking like that? .... *Turn to page 18.*

Not a fucking vegetarian? .... *Turn to page 12.*

Don't let the angel music and epic chants distract you from cooking up some holy fucking Pork Tenderloin with Fennel

1 teaspoon fennel seeds
1 pork tenderloin
Salt and pepper
3 tablespoons extra-virgin
olive oil
2 medium fennel bulbs,
diced, fronds chopped
and reserved

4 cloves garlic, minced
¼ cup Chardonnay
½ cup chicken stock
½ teaspoon fresh lemon juice
¼ cup unsalted butter

First things first, Champ: preheat your oven to 350°F. Crush your fennel seeds like they talked back to you, and then sprinkle them on the pork with some salt and pepper. Heat oil in an oven-safe sauté pan over high heat, and brown the fuck out of the pork on all sides. Haul that shit out of there and set aside. Add the fennel to the pan for about five minutes; then add the garlic and cook for one more minute. Add the booze and chicken stock to the pan, drop the pork on top of it, and roast in the oven until the pork reaches an internal temperature of 140°F to 145°F, about 15 to 20 minutes. Pull your pork out and let it rest. Put the pan with the fennel mixture back on high heat, and stir in the lemon juice and fennel fronds. Let the mixture reduce for a few minutes, and then stir in the butter. To serve, slice the fucking pork, and serve with the fennel sauce. Say grace to the mighty pig god.

Don't fucking like that? . . . . *Turn to page 16.*
Don't fucking eat meat? . . . . *Turn to page 32.*

When takeout leaves your soul feeling vacuous and estranged, make some fucking

Watermelon Salad with Ricotta Salata

¼ cup balsamic vinegar
¼ cup brown sugar
A fucking seedless
   watermelon

4 ounces ricotta
   salata
Salt and pepper
5 ounces baby arugula

Watermelon and cheese sounds about as good as church without alcohol, but guess what? You're wrong.

In a saucepan over medium heat, bring the balsamic vinegar and sugar to a boil. Lower the heat and simmer it until it's all fucking syrupy and delicious.

Cut your watermelon into cubes, and slice the ricotta salata all thin-like. Plate the watermelon and cheese together, and season those motherfuckers. Drizzle with the reduced vinegar and top with some baby arugula, and boom—you're fucking done.

Don't fucking like that? .... *Turn to page 72.*

Not a fucking vegetarian? .... *Turn to page 98.*

If you're sick, quit being a pussy. If you're not sick, enjoy some fucking Chicken Soup

A chicken, 2 to 5 pounds
2 yellow onions
4 parsnips
1 rutabaga
1 large turnip
2 ribs celery
6 carrots, divided

6 tablespoons chopped fresh parsley
6 tablespoons chopped fresh dill, divided
Salt and pepper
1 zucchini

This soup is like Jewish penicillin, if Jewish penicillin took steroids and tasted fucking amazing. Place 4 quarts of water and the chicken in a big stockpot, and bring the water to a boil. Add the whole onions, parsnips, rutabaga, turnip, celery, 4 carrots, parsley, 4 tablespoons of fresh dill, and some fucking salt and pepper. Cover that shit up and simmer it for about 3 hours. Strain the whole mixture, reserving the chicken and throwing out the vegetables. Refrigerate the stock overnight if you can; if not, then refrigerate for as long as fucking possible.

Still with me, Champ? Sure you are. When the broth is cold, skim the fat off the top and discard. Drop the stock into a pot and heat that shit back up; bring it to a boil. Shred the chicken meat, and drop it the fuck in. Dice the remaining 2 carrots and the zucchini and drop those in, too. Cook. Add the rest of the fresh dill, season that shit to taste, and serve.

Don't fucking like that? .... *Turn to page 46.*

Don't fucking eat meat? .... *Turn to page 8.*

Draw some positive attention toward yourself for a change and cook up some fucking Sage Grilled Cheese

5 tablespoons unsalted
   butter, divided
4 sprigs fresh sage, divided
4 slices country white bread,
   sliced

Salt and pepper
6 ounces fontina cheese

In a frying pan over medium heat, heat 4 tablespoons of butter until it browns, add half the fucking sage, take the pan off the heat, and let the brown butter and the sage do their thing. Coat each slice of bread on both sides with the rest of the butter and some salt and pepper. Chiffonade the remaining sage and divide it and the cheese among your sandwiches. Almost there, Sport.

Discard the sage leaves from the pan, return the pan to the heat, and drop in the sandwiches. Let those bitches get nice and brown. Flip them, cover the pan, and cook for 2 more minutes. Slice that shit in half and fucking enjoy.

Don't fucking like that? .... *Turn to page 30.*

Not a fucking vegetarian? .... *Turn to page 78.*

Don't be one of those pussies who claims vegetarian status but eats fish. Commit one way or the other, preferably on the side of meat. Oh, and eat some fucking **Seared Tuna with Citrus Sauce**

2½ cups fresh orange
    juice
3 tablespoons lemon juice
2 tablespoons lime juice
½ cup soy sauce
1 tablespoon balsamic
    vinegar
1 tablespoon sesame oil

2-inch piece fresh ginger,
    peeled and sliced
4 tuna steaks
1 tablespoon Chinese
    five-spice powder
Salt and pepper
3 tablespoons extra-virgin
    olive oil

In a saucepan, combine the juices, soy sauce, vinegar, oil, and ginger, and simmer 15 minutes. Strain the fucking sauce. Season the tuna with the Chinese five-spice powder and salt and pepper: coat that shit on all sides.

In a nonstick skillet, heat the olive oil over high heat, get the pan hot as fuck, then add the tuna. Sear for 1 minute per side, then stop. If you don't stop, you have ruined a nice piece of fish, and you don't want that weighing on your conscience. Slice the tuna and spoon on the sauce, then eat that shit.

Don't fucking like that? . . . . *Turn to page 34.*
Don't fucking eat meat? . . . . *Turn to page 54.*

Bonjour mon ami de culinaire, faisez quelque fucking Tomatoes Provençal

6 tomatoes
Salt and pepper
¾ cup fresh bread crumbs
¼ cup chopped fresh parsley

1 tablespoon minced garlic
3 tablespoons extra-virgin
   olive oil

Get your oven hot: 350°F if you want to fucking split hairs. Halve the tomatoes and season them with salt and pepper. Set them on a baking sheet.

Mix the bread crumbs, parsley, and garlic together, and season to taste with some more salt and pepper. Make sure the seasoning is perfect, because if it's not, everyone will judge you, even if they deny it. Coat your tomatoes with the mixture, and then drizzle in olive oil.

Bake for about 20 minutes, or until perfectly golden brown, fucking huge emphasis on "perfectly."

Don't fucking like that? .... *Turn to page 56.*

Not a fucking vegetarian? .... *Turn to page 92.*

Make your fat ass fatter with some fucking Shrimp and Grits

3 cups milk

2 cloves garlic, minced and divided

Salt and pepper

¾ cup grits

6 slices good bacon, chopped

1½ pounds large shrimp

3 large shallots, finely chopped

2 cups baby arugula

2 tablespoons extra-virgin olive oil

1 lemon

Bring the milk to a boil in a saucepan with half the garlic and some salt and pepper. Whisk in the grits, reduce the heat to medium-low, and simmer that bitch until the grits are tender and creamy. Don't forget to stir that shit constantly; nobody said this would be easy. When they're cooked, season to taste. Cook the bacon in a skillet until crisp and perfect: honor this holy beast. Set the blessed bacon aside. Sauté the salted and peppered shrimp in the bacon fat until they are pink: this shit only takes a minute. Add the shallots and remaining garlic, and cook for another minute. Put some grits on a plate, throw some chopped bacon on top, throw some shrimp on top of that, throw some baby arugula on top of that, and then give that shit a golden shower of olive oil and the juice of the lemon.

Don't fucking like that? . . . . *Turn to page 68.*

Don't fucking eat meat? . . . . *Turn to page 60.*

Your dreadlocks and hacky sack are charming, but I digress: cook up some fucking Vegetarian Cassoulet

2 tablespoons extra-virgin
   olive oil
2 zucchini, diced
2 ribs celery, diced
1 white onion, diced
Salt and pepper
4 cloves garlic, sliced

2 cups diced Roma tomatoes
3 cups cooked cannellini
   beans
4 sprigs fresh thyme
4 sprigs fresh rosemary
2 bay leaves
Some fucking bread

Preheat your oven to 400°F. Heat the oil in a large
skillet over medium heat, add the zucchini, celery,
and onion, and cook until caramelized and soft, about 8
minutes. I'll come to your house and shank you if you
don't fucking season your vegetables. Mix in the garlic,
and cook for another minute. Don't get all distracted and
let it cook for more: it will get bitter and taste like shit.

Combine the vegetables, tomatoes, beans, thyme,
rosemary, and bay leaves in a casserole dish. Bake for
about 30 minutes, or until when you taste it, you explode
in your pants. Remove the bay leaves and serve with
bread.

Don't fucking like that? .... *Turn to page 96.*
Not a fucking vegetarian? .... *Turn to page 36.*

Make your urine smell delightfully awkward with some fucking Asparagus with Egg

1 pound asparagus
2 tablespoons grated
    Parmesan cheese

Salt and pepper
2 tablespoons butter
Some fucking eggs

Cook your asparagus however the fuck you want. Grilling it is ace, but blanching will work too. Either way, season it with plenty of salt and pepper. Seriously, don't be a pussy. When it's properly cooked, sprinkle the grated Parmesan cheese over it, and let that shit get all fucking melty.

In a frying pan, heat the butter over medium heat. Crack the eggs into the pan and season them with salt and pepper; cook until the whites are set. Flip it if you want. I truly don't give a shit about your egg proclivities: that's between you and God. Serve the asparagus with an egg on top, easy as fuck.

Don't fucking like that? .... *Turn to page 26.*
Not a fucking vegetarian? .... *Turn to page 28.*

If halibut could cook, it would make you, so return the favor and make some fucking Grilled Halibut

1 jalapeño pepper
1 garlic clove
2 red bell peppers
4 cups extra-virgin olive oil,
    divided
Salt and pepper

2 teaspoons ground cumin,
    divided
2 teaspoons ground
    coriander, divided
4 halibut fillets
1 lemon, sliced

Get your grill hot as balls. Skewer the jalapeño, garlic, and red bell pepper and douse them in oil and some salt and pepper. Grill those bitches until they are charred and tender. When they're ready, and not a fucking second before, peel the charred skin off, core, and seed them. Blend them with 2 tablespoons of olive oil and 1 teaspoon each of cumin and coriander. And I know you didn't forget to season with salt and pepper to taste. Get that shit smooth. Drizzle the remaining oil on the fish, then season it on both sides with rest of the cumin, coriander, salt, and pepper. Grill it for 4 minutes per side; don't overcook it, and don't fucking move it too much. Let some lemon slices keep it company on the grill; the halibut is a social fish. Serve the fish over the sauce, and squeeze some grilled lemon juice on it.

Don't fucking like that? .... *Turn to page 62.*
Don't fucking eat meat? .... *Turn to page 80.*

Your reverse Midas touch turns everything to shit, but how about trying not to fuck up some fucking Pork Loin with Peach Compote

4 cloves garlic

1 tablespoon fresh minced
    ginger

1 teaspoon curry powder

Salt and pepper

A fucking pork tenderloin

1 medium white onion, diced

2 tablespoons extra-virgin
    olive oil

1 cup diced cherry tomatoes

1 peach, diced

2 teaspoons fresh thyme

Preheat your oven to 425°F. Mash the garlic, ginger, curry powder, and some salt and pepper into a paste. I don't give a fuck how you choose to do this; just make it a paste. Rub that shit all over the pork. Yeah, you like that, don't you? Add the oil to a Dutch oven over high heat, and brown the shit out of the tenderloin. Transfer the pork to the oven and cook it until its internal temperature is 140°F, about 15 to 20 minutes; let it rest, and it will come to the necessary temperature to not kill you. For the compote, add the onion to the pan and sauté that shit over high heat for about 5 minutes. Make it rain tomatoes and peaches, and sauté those motherfuckers for another 4 minutes, then add the thyme. Slice the pork and serve with the peach compote.

Don't fucking like that? . . . . *Turn to page 4.*

Don't fucking eat meat? . . . . *Turn to page 66.*

Watch this, I'm a fucking mind reader: you are going to make some fucking Linguine with Snap Peas, Ricotta, and Mint

12 ounces linguine

1 cup sugar snap peas

¼ cup chopped fresh basil

¼ cup chopped fresh mint

½ cup ricotta2 teaspoons
extra-virgin olive oil

¼ cup grated Parmesan
cheese

1 tablespoon lemon juice

Salt and pepper

Bring some salty-ass water to boil and cook the pasta perfectly; don't fuck up, Tough Guy. While the pasta is cooking, trim the ends of the snap peas, and cut them in half. To the perfectly-cooked pasta, add the snap peas, basil, and mint, and give that shit a golden shower of olive oil. Toss to mix, then add the cheeses and mix those up. Add the lemon juice and some salt and pepper to taste; don't be a pussy about the seasoning, or your food will suck, and you can't put that one on me.

Don't fucking like that? . . . . *Turn to page 84.*

Not a fucking vegetarian? . . . . *Turn to page 50.*

Fuck that diet you've been talking about for three years, cook up some fucking Chicken Provençal

4 tomatoes, cut into wedges
1 white onion, cut into
    wedges
½ cup black olives
4 cloves garlic, sliced and
    divided
¼ cup extra-virgin olive oil,
    divided

2 teaspoons herbes de
    Provence, divided
1 teaspoon fennel seeds
Salt and pepper
A fucking chicken, trussed

Preheat your oven to 425°F, Champ. In a baking dish, toss together the tomatoes, onion, olives, half of the garlic, 2 tablespoons of oil, 1 teaspoon herbes de Provence, the fennel seeds, and some salt and pepper. Make a well for the chicken in the middle; that way, its fucking meatpieces will make the vegetables taste better. Stir together the rest of the garlic, the remaining teaspoon of herbes de Provence, the remaining olive oil, and some salt and pepper. Dump that shit on the trussed chicken and rub it all over. Yeah, you like that. Bake that shit until the chicken is at 100°F, about an hour, but don't count on your timer: stay on top of that shit. When it's ready, let it rest for about 10 minutes. Don't fucking slice it yet or I'll cut you. Serve with the vegetables, and fucking voilà.

Don't fucking like that? .... *Turn to page 44.*
Don't fucking eat meat? .... *Turn to page 88.*

Procure some child labor to cheaply and efficiently cook up some fucking
Salmon with Honey and Soy

4 salmon fillets
3 cloves garlic, minced
½ cup soy sauce
2 tablespoons honey

2 tablespoons sesame oil
1 lemon
Salt and pepper

Marinate the salmon with the minced garlic, soy sauce, honey, sesame oil, and the juice from the lemon. Let that shit sit for at least an hour.

Turn on your broiler. Season the fish and broil until medium-rare, or if you're a pussy, however overcooked you enjoy it: about 5 minutes for non-pussy cooking.

Don't fucking like that? .... *Turn to page 42.*

Don't fucking eat meat? .... *Turn to page 53.*